The Japanese Bath

BRUCE SMITH
YOSHIKO YAMAMOTO

GIBBS·SMITH
P
PUBLISHER

Salt Lake City

On the cover: A private residence's wood-heated bath in the Sierra foothills of northern California.

Opposite title page: Bath at Nagaza Inn, Gifu Prefecture, Japan.

Title page: Stools and a wooden tub for bathing in the Kodakara-yu Sento at the Edo-Tokyo Open Air Architectural Museum in Japan.

First Edition
13 12 11 10   13 12 11 10 9 8

Published by
Gibbs Smith, Publisher
P. O. Box 667
Layton, UT 84041

Orders: (1-800) 748-5439
Visit our Web site at www.gibbs-smith.com

Photographic Credits
Photos by Bruce Smith: pages 1–4, 6–8, 13–16, 18–20, 22–26, 28, 29, 34–36, 42, 44, 47, 49, 51, 54–58, 60, 61, 63, 65–68, 71, 79, 84, 88, 90, and 96. Photos by Bruce Smith and Aya Brackett: front cover, 17, 27, 59 62, 69, 70, 74, and 76. Photos by Aya Brackett: 5, 41 and 75. Photos by Michael Chase, courtesy Ki Arts: 21, 53, and 83. All other photos courtesy as per captions.

Designed by Trice Boerens and Cherie Hanson of B Design
Edited by Gail Yngve
Printed in Hong Kong

Library of Congress Cataloging-in-Publication Data

Smith, Bruce

    The Japanese bath / by Bruce Smith and Yoshiko Yamamato.— 1st ed.
      p.cm
    ISBN 1-58685-027-X — 978-1-58685-027-2

    1. Bathing customs—Japan. 2. Baths—Japan. I. Yamamoto, Yoshiko.
II. Title.

GT2846.J3 S6 2001
391.6'4—dc21

00-011750

Dedication
To Hidemi and Yukiko Yamamoto and
Hideko, Kazuhiko, Kento, and Reina Yamamoto,
who have shared with us
the most precious time
of bath and bathing

Basukurin, a bath soap produced by Tsumura in the 1930s.

In the lonely mountain
water is overflowing over the tub—
steam of this hot springs
is thicker than the mountain fog
—*Yosano Akiko*

Contents

Acknowledgments

Shop display of handcrafted tubs by Arai Shuichi, Kawagoe, Japan.

As the pleasure of bathing in a public *sento* in Japan comes from sharing the bath water with others, so has much of the pleasure of researching and writing this book come from the time shared with the many people who helped, encouraged, guided, and supported our vision of this project.

In particular, we would like to give thanks to Laura Voisin George, who devoted so much research time to us, finding many sources and homes for the book. We are grateful to Steve Fletcher, Carl Croft, Delwin Rimbey, and their staff at Dandelion, who not only lent us objects for our photo shoots but also shared Yakedono, their beautiful home with a serene Japanese bath set on a northern California mountaintop. We give heartfelt thanks to Arai Shuichi in Kawagoe, Japan, who granted us an unforgettable afternoon showing us each and every step of making a traditional Japanese tub, and to Duke Klauck and Julia Goldberg at Ten Thousand Waves, who with Gibbs Smith had the original vision for this book. We were fortunate to work with two very talented young photographers: Aya Brackett and Rebecca Kent each contributing vastly to the quality of the images used in this book. We are indebted to Dakota Eckard and Ursula Dawkins for their assistance in finding models. We thank Chadine Flood Gong of Chadine Interior Design, Jimmy Maekawa of Japan Woodworking & Design, and Glen Collins of Hana Shoji and Interiors for their patience with our questions and for their assistance in finding homes to photograph. Ed Stiles not only allowed us to photograph his home and led us to another wonderful bath to photograph, he also gave us invaluable information regarding the history of the Japanese bath in America. The time we spent with Len Brackett at his home and workplace in the Sierra foothills opened our eyes to a sense of refined Japanese simplicity that is possible but rarely achieved in this country.

We are also grateful to many individuals at various Japanese institutions and companies, whose generosities we wish we could return someday: Edo-Tokyo Museum, Saitama Prefectural Museum, Tokyo Public Bath Association, archives at Kao Corporation, Daikoku-yu in Tokyo, Kaho in Nigata Prefecture, Sansuiso in Fukushima Prefecture, Hogetsu in Hakone area, Yunogo-mura in Shuzenji Hot Springs, Gorokaku in Gumma Prefecture, Hoeiso in Hakone, Kona Hotel in Izu-Nagaoka area, Kindai Pension in Gumma Prefecture, Tenoji-ya in Kusatsu Hot Springs, Otakino-yu in Kusatsu, Nagaya at Fukuchi Hot Springs, Nanadaru Hot Springs in Shizuoka Prefecture, Kodai Hinoki, Kiso Artech, Hinoki Soken, INAX, and Tsumura.

We also wish to acknowledge and give thanks to a number of individuals and organizations who helped us in our writing, research, and photography: Beverly Hot Springs; Mike Chase; East Wind (Higashikaze) Inc.; Masaru Seido at Gilroy Hot Springs; Ron Herman, Landscape Architect; Hida Tools; Paul Discoe and Gloria McMillan at Joinery Structures; Kathy Nelson at Kabuki Hot Springs and Spa; Ann and Hiroshi Sakaguchi at Ki Arts; Karen Ray and Michael Stusser at Osmosis Enzyme Bath and Massage; Robert Ghelertel at Robert's Hot Tubs; Bill Findley at Sea Otter Wood Works; Leslie and everyone else at Tassajara Zen Mountain Center; Jacqueline Sa at Tea Garden Springs, who guided us as to the health benefits of bathing; Kayt Cunningham, Greg Lopatosky, and Kartar Kaur at Ten Thousand Waves, who introduced us to Herbal Wraps, Watsu, and Salt Glows; Thousand Cranes Futon Shop; Norm Potter and Bill McCaulay of Tubmakers; Annette Curi at the Hannah Carter Japanese Garden of the University of California, Los Angeles; Watercourse Way; Matthew Kondo and Jane Lee at San Francisco's Hotel Nikko; Gene and Diep Agress; Michael Andrews and Celeste Weidman; Brenda and Jeff Bohn; Leslie Desmond for her enthusiasm; Betty and Elliot Finkle; Everal Mitchell; Keiko Nelson; Kent and Fumiko Singleton; Robert and Carol Swenson; Yoshiko Wada and Hercules Morphopoulos; and Joseph and Kimiko Wilkerson.

We were fortunate to have the courageous participation of models willing to soak for three and sometimes four hours in the lukewarm water of a Japanese bathtub just so we could achieve that perfect photograph. We give thanks to Lara Tran, Alexander, Ariel, and Max Agress; Tamara Alvarez, Ursula Dawkins, Angela Pitu, Laura Rainville, and Cathy Vu—who traveled all the way from Seattle just for this project; Kento Yamamoto, Ceaser Zepeda, Leilani Buddenhagen, and Priscilla Freeman.

The vision for this project was enabled as always by the support and encouragement of our talented, disciplinarian editor, Gail Yngve. We value her more than we can express.

This *kasuga* lantern is seen in the garden outside the Kodakara-yu Sento at the Edo-Tokyo Open Air Architectural Museum in Japan.

Introduction

We have lived our lives outside of Japan for more than a decade now. One of us was born in the center of Tokyo; the other merely lived and worked in Japan for four years. Yet, wherever we are now, wherever we live, work, or travel, we both carry elements of that culture that we count as essential to the way we want to live. At home, we eat at least once a week a meal of *soba*, the buckwheat noodles that are served in hot broth during winter and cold in summer, carefully arranged on a bamboo tray. We value in others that essential part of Japanese communication that places the obligation upon the listener to understand all that cannot be directly said by the speaker. And nightly, we try to bring an end to the mad whirl of the day by slowly, carefully sinking into the hot water of a bath.

We intensely miss the experience of the bath in Japan—to be precise, though, it is not the bath but bathing that we miss. Whether it was taking a bath in a modern fiberglass-molded unit bath in a Tokyo high-rise, or soaking in the wooden tubs of a public bath in the deep mountainside of Shinshu, our memories of the bath and bathing are not about rooms and architecture. They are about entering quiet spaces, splashing water over the back, scrubbing one's feet or helping an older lady wash her back, then slowly descending into the steaming water, sitting next to a stranger and exchanging smiles and sharing thoughts, and, finally, getting dressed in street wear or a *yukata*, a lightweight cotton summer kimono, and entering the world again refreshed and renewed.

This is not to say that the Japanese bath has no distinct architectural features. As we will explain in this book, many important and some minor differences distinguish Japanese from Western bath—preeminently the idea that washing is something separate from soaking. But understanding the Japanese bath is like understanding what it takes to bake great bread; it takes far more than just a good recipe. Turning out the quintessential loaf takes having a life that is centered around cooking and eating and the sharing of food—a life where the crusty smell coming out of the hot oven brings joy, where the handing of a piece of buttered hot bread to a loved one becomes essential to good living. So it is with the bath. One cannot simply add a wooden bathtub to a home and believe he or she is having a Japanese experience. It is the totality of life around the bath that makes a bath Japanese.

Our purposes in this book are both to introduce and explain the Japanese bath, and then to convey an understanding of all that cannot be usually stated about the bath as a state of mind, its relation to nature, its place in a family and a community, its sensuality and wholesomeness, its structure and craft, and the joy it can bring to one's life.

Evening time in the rustic *rotenburo*, the outdoor
bath at Hoei-so Inn in Hakone, Japan.

Bathing

It is just on the edge of evening. You have been surrounded
by the push and bustle of people all day, and, finally, just now,
you have returned home. Stopping to listen, you hear the late-
afternoon breeze in the tall pine tree outside. You sit quietly on
the back porch, peel and eat a tangerine, then walk a short while
in your garden. Back inside, your clothing comes off easily and
you put on a lightweight *yukata*. Walking to the bathhouse
through the corridor overlooking the garden, you reach down to
check the water temperature in the bath, then look up to see
out the window and through the trees that the sun is just settling down between the distant hills. You hang the *yukata* on a
hook and sit on a wooden stool in the washing area; you are
now at the right height to look directly out into the trees. With
the wooden bucket, you scoop water from the tub and pour it
over yourself, rinsing off all the noise and bother of the day. You
do this twice more, making sure that when you step into the
bath, you will not carry with you any dirt or refuse. You lower
yourself into the bath as the last sliver of the sun drops below
the hills, then stay there ten, maybe fifteen, minutes, watching
the colors change, grow in intensity, then settle back into a
warm softness. Stepping again into the washing area, you scrub
your body, starting with your hair, your ears, your neck, working
your way down to your toes. After rinsing carefully, once again
you sit back into the bath. It is growing dark now and suddenly
seems quieter. Just barely you can hear the sound of the breeze.

Protected by bamboo, the path winds towards the wooden Japanese gate at Osmosis in Freestone, California.

Entry

Entering a bath in Japan is to enter another world. It is a place where one not only cleans the body but also cleanses the mind. Unlike Western bathrooms, Japanese bathing rooms are entirely separate from the toilet—they are independent spaces reserved only for the daily task of taking a bath, cleaning oneself, and relaxing. They are places one enters with deliberation and anticipation.

The traditional Japanese domestic bathroom was usually located at the end of a hallway or was sited in a structure entirely independent from the main house. One would be intensely aware of the carefully constructed garden views when walking to and from the bath, something considered an integral part of the bathing experience. Since each household had only one bathroom (if, indeed, there was any), the room for bathing was separate, not just from the toilet, but from the bedroom. Unlike in traditional Western cultures, it was treated as an independent component of the house—as distinct and important, for example, as the kitchen. And like the kitchen, it was an area of the house in which strength of the family's life could be measured—by the sharing of the bathwater, the order in which each person took his or her bath, and the way thoughts and concerns difficult to speak of elsewhere could be mentioned there.

Still today, one can find in *ryokans* (traditional Japanese inns) the communal bath located at the end of an *engawa*, a long corridor or veranda providing an interim space between the inside and the outside. Psychologically there is something very centering and calming about this walk to the bath. Walking slowly there in a lightweight, cleanly starched *yukata* builds up the anticipation for a wonderful, relaxing meditation in the hot water.

The broad overhang of the roof creates a space neither inside nor outside in this northern California house.

The transition into a massage
room is gradual and gentle
at Ten Thousand Waves,
Santa Fe, New Mexico.

Seated in the *engawa*, one can feel part of the garden in this residence south of San Francisco.

The *engawa* is usually made of beautifully grained wood or bamboo and is raised about twenty inches above the ground. In warm weather, it will be opened totally to the outside; in the cool autumn or snowy winter, a set of glass or wooden sliding doors running along the outer edge will be pulled shut to preserve the inner heat of the house. The *engawa* is protected from sunlight and rain by the eaves of the roof.

The ingenuity of *engawa* is in its connecting the interior of the home to the outside world; it is neither inside nor out. The materials chosen for this area reflect the transitional character of this space; wood and bamboo are more durable than softer materials, such as the *shoji* paper and *tatami* mats, used inside, and are often left unpolished, retaining a rustic quality.

Trees protect the
quiet path leading
to the guest cottage
with a Japanese
bath in this north-
ern California
home.

Entering the Daikokuya Sento in Tokyo, a bather must duck under the *noren*.

At the *sento* (the public bath), on the other hand, there is no such corridor for the bathers—coming to the *sento* is not about the transition from public to private but rather about the shift from the outside world into a community. Stepping inside off the street, one passes through an entrance that has the auspicious appearance of a temple because of its roofing structure, called a *karahafu*. All that separates the outside world from the inner entry is a cotton or linen *noren* (cloth screen) hanging over the threshold. Bathers step in, duck under it, and take off their shoes inside before paying their bath fee to the attendant. Something about this action of ducking under the *noren* marks the beginning of the bathing experience, indicating that a bather has now stepped away from the outside world. By the time one adjusts his or her eyes to the interior darkness and the sound of gushing water, clonking buckets, and talking people, one is ready to relax and join the community of bathers.

Kodakara-yu Sento at Edo-Tokyo Open
Air Architectural Museum in Tokyo, with
its prominent *karahafu* roof structure.

An antique lattice-work door separates the *datsuiba* from the *hinoki* bath in this Berkeley, California, residence.

The Datsuiba

A *datsuiba* with a washstand designed and constructed by Ki Arts of Occidental, California.

Before entering the bathing room, one must pass first through the *datsuiba* (changing room). Like the *engawa* that separates the outside world from the inner sanctuary of the home, the *datsuiba* provides a transition space between the watery world of the bath and the dry world of the house. Usually equipped with a small cosmetic stand, sink, and mirror, the *datsuiba* provides a comfortable space for taking off one's clothes, and for drying off and putting on fresh clothes after the bath. In contrast to the inner world of the bathing area that is designed to be drenched with water, the *datsuiba* is kept dry and clean. Often in the modern Japanese home, the washing machine and dryer are located here. It is here also that the family members will wash their hands, brush their teeth, and comb their hair.

In private homes, the *datsuiba* can be as small as five by eight feet—in contrast, in *sento* or *onsen* (public baths or hot-spring resorts) needing to accommodate many bathers at once, it can be as enormous as thirty by forty feet. Ubiquitous to *datsuiba* of any size, though, are the scales for bathers to measure their weight each and every time they visit the baths.

The door between the *datsuiba* and the bathroom is usually made of glass, often frosted. The reasons are twofold: first, if somebody is using the bath, another member of the family can use the *datsuiba* without disturbing the bather, and also, the glass allows light to enter the *datsuiba* from the bathing area, where almost always natural light pours in from a window placed over the tub. Especially for the elderly, Japanese are careful to keep the *datsuiba* area warm during the cold seasons since a great difference in temperature between the bathroom and the *datsuiba* can cause a sudden increase in blood pressure. Often they will have a heater in this room to ensure a warm area for changing and getting ready for the bath.

The large *datsuiba* can accommodate forty to fifty people at Kodakara-yu Sento, Tokyo Open Air Architecture Museum.

22

The Outside within the Inside

It could be said that the innermost room of the Japanese house is the room with the bath, yet one finds many gentle reminders and references to the world beyond. As mentioned above, almost always there is a window to the outside set right above the tub. When the home has a substantial garden space, often the windows are large and able to be opened out into the garden. The bath then becomes part of the changing seasons. In spring, one enjoys gazing at the fragile white petals of plum and watching the cherry blossoms fall; in summer, the rich green wisteria leaves threaten to climb through the window into the bathroom; in autumn, while taking a bath, one can watch

With skylights above and a porch opening to the outside, nature becomes part of the bathing experience at Ten Thousand Waves, Santa Fe, New Mexico.

how the brilliantly colored Japanese maples darken in color day by day; and, in winter, the perfect complement to a hot steamy bath is the cold wind that brushes through the bare silvery branches covered with crisp white snow.

A view from the bath is important, but so is privacy, especially if one cannot have the luxury of spaciousness. To protect the view out, especially when looking into a neighbor's yard, fences made of natural materials like cedar, redwood, and bamboo can create a visual border and a sense of protection. Better yet, planting hedges, trees, and bamboo right outside the bath window can create a softer and pleasing protective barrier—a living fence, so to speak. These fences can

face various directions. The obvious direction is one parallel to the bathroom window, directly protecting the view from the opposite side. Another option often used in the Japanese home is to build the fence out from the side of the house. Called a *sode-gaki*, a sleeve fence, these low fences—only four to five feet high and butting out only two to four feet from the house—are often ornamental but can also help obstruct unwanted views.

Another way to allow the outside in yet retain privacy, especially when the window is not facing a garden, is to either pane the window with opaque glass or to use glass inspired by *shoji* screens that creates a soft boundary to the outside with its white luminescent quality. Here, it is the suggestion of the natural world that is enjoyed. A tree placed outside, even in a container, will allow

A wooden fence defines outdoor space in the same way a wall defines indoor space in this northern California residence.

Here at a public bath in Tokyo, the real world of nature is close at hand while visions of an ideal Japanese outdoors is portrayed in the traditional mural above the huge soaking tub.

The windows of this northern California bath are set low and covered with *sudare*, defining the garden view seen while bathing in a *hinoki* bathtub.

Shadows on frosted glass reflect the natural world outside in this light and airy northern Californian bathroom.

the sun to cast dark and light shadows of branches swaying in the wind on the glass—almost as though a quiet shadow play were being performed. As the novelist Tanizaki Jun'ichiro wrote in his essay "In Praise of Shadows," "a Japanese room depends on a variation of shadows, heavy shadows against light shadows—it has nothing else."

When deciding about glass and views, try actually sitting inside the bathtub and in the washing area to see which area of the exterior truly needs to be eliminated from view. Surprisingly, very little actually needs to be screened off in most cases. And the amount of frosting on the glass should be kept to a minimum because it is vital to allow the warmth of the light to come through—in a manner reminiscent of Japanese *washi* paper held up against the sun.

In extreme situations where privacy is a dire issue, one can consider lowering the line of vision out of the window all the way down to just one or two feet from the ground. Often seen in traditional Japanese homes with *tatami* mats, where people sit low to the ground, this type of low window creates a dramatic effect, immediately connecting the viewer to an intimate garden of rocks, moss, and lanterns.

The colors of the exterior
wall and the bamboo
complement the soft
color of the Port Orford
cedar used for the *ofuro*
in this California home.

Generous use of glass allows a bath
to seem set in the garden in this Palo
Alto, California, home.

A carefully created garden is a micro-cosm of the natural world when the elements of water, trees, stone, and sky are used as in this elegant Japanese garden at Osmosis in Freestone, California.

Created Scenery

More than establishing privacy by building walls, the essence of traditional Japanese architecture is the construction of a place from which the world can be viewed—even when the presentation of the outside world is merely an ideal representation rather than the reality. One technique is the enclosure of the outside. When applied to the bath, this would mean that rather than having a window opening out onto a grand vista, one would choose to focus the attention of the bather on a carefully constructed small garden—a space delicately defined and composed into an idealized microcosmos. An intimate space of this type is often seen in private homes and *sentos*. When done with consideration, this garden can be viewed not only from the bath but also from the sitting area where bathers cool themselves after a long hot soak by sipping cold drinks as they sit comfortably looking out onto the garden space. The gardens at *sentos* are usually located just outside the changing area—one for each sex. Though it is a small space, often no larger than a small garage, it brings into this innermost world the fresh air of the outside along with an idealized scene of the world beyond.

To create this type of enclosed garden, one needs first to establish a clear boundary by setting up ornamental fences, plantings, walls, and screens. Then, working within this small, now-defined space, a few carefully selected materials are arranged: moss and miniature pine trees, stone lanterns and rocks, concrete basins and smooth pebbles. All are used to create a small symbolic world. It is important to carefully choose the size of these plantings and objects, since each item should not only suggest an element in nature but also retain harmony with the other items and the scale of the world being created. Carefully constructed, this miniature landscape can suggest an intricate world of natural elements, allowing viewers to wander through hills, forests, and along rivers while merely looking out the window of their bath.

Carefully selected stones—by their sizes, shapes, and quality—can repre-
sent scenes of ocean, river, valley, marsh, and waving reeds. To create a
scene of the ocean, a Heian-period text instructs one to

A *rotenburo* at Kona-besso in
Shizuoka Prefecture, Japan.

> . . . *first construct the scene of a rough seashore, placing some*
> *pointed rocks in a casual looking manner. Then place a sequence*
> *of rocks from the shore toward the offing, making them appear as*
> *though they extend from the shore. There should be a few rocks*
> *isolated from the rest. As these rocks are ruthlessly exposed to the*
> *billows, they should look like they had been washed out. Finally*
> *you should provide here and there views of the sandbank and*
> *white beach where some black pines may be planted. . . .*

Or to create a landscape of waving
reeds, one is instructed to place stones

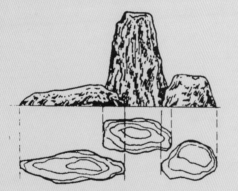

> . . . *here and there towards the end of the hillside field or at the*
> *pond shore, and . . . associated with low plants such as the*
> *grass bamboo, mountain sedge and the like. As for the trees to*
> *be planted, preferences should be given to those of soft forms like*
> *the plum tree and the weeping willow. As a rule, flat stones are*
> *used for this style of landscape. . . .*

In arranging these objects, the goal is to suggest nature, rather than to copy it or control it.

A *rotenburo* made of stone at Nanadaru in Shizuoka Prefecture, Japan.

Practical Hints for Creating a Small Rock Garden

The placement of stones in front of the bathhouse at the Tassajara Zen Center, California, defines the pathway to the entrance.

The Surface of a Stone: It is better to choose a stone that retains its original natural quality rather than one that has been polished, carved, or otherwise finished by human hands.

The Shape of a Stone: Though stones come in every shape and size, generally they can be classed as vertical, horizontal, or intermediary, which would include round and slanted stones. The groupings of shapes should be carefully considered.

The Colors of a Stone: Stones can be divided into color groups: red, blue, black, and so on. It is better to stay within one color group to retain visual harmony.

The Direction of Grain in a Stone: A stone's character comes from the patterns and grain that run along its surface. This gives force and direction to the stone.

The Hardness of a Stone: The harder the stone is, the more worthy it is.

The _Chi_ of a Stone: All of these qualities listed above make up a stone and give it a particular _chi_. To understand this _chi_ is very important in correctly using the stone.

Landscaping with One Stone:

Put the stone at a focal point in the garden. Do not randomly place it or simply set it in a convenient location. Bury it in the ground so that it looks as though it is showing only a part of itself. When used as a flat, horizontal shape, it gives a peaceful and stable feeling. When used vertically, it gives an upward force to the garden.

A stone anchors both the man-made and natural elements next to this outdoor bath in Occidental, California.

Landscaping with Two or More Stones:

- The fewer the stones used, the more restrained the expression will be.

- Do not mix different types of stone qualities.

- If using two stones, make sure to use different shapes and sizes.

- Make sure that the spatial relationship between the two stones is pleasant.

- Never put two stones side by side in a straight line.

- The most popular, the three-stone composition, should always have stones that are different in height, often with the tallest one in the middle.

A *yukimi* lantern is set appropriately
next to this *rotenburo* at Nanadaru,
Shizuoka Prefecture, Japan.

Some Hints on Using Stone Lanterns

Stone lanterns, originally used as symbolic offerings in Buddhist and Shintoist traditions, were later incorporated by tea masters for their tea gardens to illuminate the pathways at night. Though they had the practical purpose of lighting the dark steps at dusk, today they are mostly used for their picturesque appearance. However, since their original purpose was illumination, it would make visual sense to try to put them in places where they would serve their original function. These lanterns include *kasuga doro*

A *rotenburo* at Kona-besso in Shizuoka Prefecture, Japan.

Kasuga doro

Okigata doro

Yukimi doro

(*kasuga*-type lantern), a formal tall lantern that requires a bigger space next to a shrub or under a tree; *okigata doro* (ground-type low lantern), which is made of only the top parts of the lantern and is often used at the turn of a pathway to light the steps; and *yukimi doro* (snow-viewing lantern), often used next to a pond or a small stream. These lanterns not only create a focal point in the view but also help humanize the feeling of the garden.

A silhouette of the mountain encloses the space as night falls at this outdoor bath at Hoei-so in Hakone, Japan.

Shakkei

Those fortunate enough to have a scene of distant trees, hills, or the silhouette of a mountain range in their landscapes can actively design such distant views into their bathing spaces. Called *shakkei*, literally translated as borrowing scenery, this ancient technique of landscape architecture was often used in Zen gardens to connect the enclosed yard to the surrounding views.

To create a *shakkei*, one must first understand the topography of the area in relation to the house and bathing area, and then create a visual barrier that eliminates unwanted views while capturing the grand backdrop beyond. To understand how much of the distant scenery is visible and to see what interference is caused by a neighbor's roofline, it helps to crouch down in the bathtub or washing area and study the view. Drawing a diagram and mapping out the angles involved often helps. Additionally, putting up a mock wall with various vertical heights can also help in imagining the type of barrier that needs to be created.

One important detail to remember while creating a *shakkei* is "the principle of the three depths," a perspective technique used by East Asian landscape painters. Unlike most Western paintings, which have a perspective constructed from a vanishing point, the East Asian technique piles one vista on top of another in three stages: the foreground, middle distance, and far distance. The viewer's eyes can move from the closest scenery of stones and moss and travel to the fence or the hedge, then extend beyond to the beautiful backdrop of waterfall or mountains. In this created scenery, a person's mind is allowed to freely travel from one's own narrow world to the distant mountains or even to the sky and clouds beyond.

Colors of the walls should complement the warmth of the *hinoki*, as used in this bath built by Kisoartech, Japan.

Color

The color palette has changed over the years in Japan. Today many Japanese favor light pastel colors, which has led to a plethora of new fiberglass and tiled baths made in light colors that range from weak mint to orange sorbet. The idea prevails now that the whiter the bathing area, the cleaner, more modern and Western it is. Many *sentos* also use a light color scheme for their interiors, often combining bright white walls with clean aqua blue for tiles on the floor. In contrast to these modern colors, *sentos* also have murals that stretch across both the men's and women's baths that are painted in bold combinations of azures, greens, and browns. Often depicting Mount Fuji behind a sandy beach with pine trees or, a little less often, a tropical island, these paintings have a folk art-like charm in presenting a stereotypical view of favored places that bring scenes of nature inside the bath house. They

also create a sense of celebration in the minds of Japanese bathers as they gaze at the scenes through the white steam of the bath.

To savor the pleasures of the bath completely, one should turn back to the traditional color palettes of Japan—and to do this, one must first grasp the concept of *shibui*. Impossible to simply define with a word, this is a concept derived from the tea ceremony. It refers to a reserved, simple, elegant, and rough quality—a kind of beauty that Boye De Menthe refers to in *Oriental Secrets of Graceful Living* as being "in perfect harmony with nature." It suggests "serenity, nobility and quiet luxury."

An all-Kiso-*hinoki* bathroom, designed and built by Hinoki Soken in Japan.

It is the opposite of vulgar displays of wealth and abundance and can be represented by colors found in unpolished gold and silver, slate and granite, ashes, the various soft greens of moss or the yellows of wild mustard. Using the dark gray of granite slate can echo the rocks placed carefully in the garden, and the rich yellow ochre of tiles can complement the warm glow of the *hinoki* wood used in making the bath. One chooses colors that enhance the materials used in the bathroom—colors that reflect the wood, tile, or stone.

The colors associated with a sense of *shibui* are tertiary or quaternary tones, the colors produced by mixing the primary tones two or three times. The more one mixes the color and moves from the primary tones, the more subdued and grayed the colors become. One can find these colors used in Japanese teahouses because they are soothing colors, far from the harshness of primary tones. As the novelist Tanizaki Jun'ichiro put it in his poetic prose: these "neutral colors" are used "so that the sad, fragile, dying rays can sink into absolute repose."

A bathroom designed and built by East Wind (Higashikaze), Inc., for a residence in the Sierra Foothills of California.

Candlelight allows a restful
darkness during bathing time
in this San Francisco residence.

With Darkness
and Without

A contemporary light is inspired by a traditional Japanese *andon*.

As with colors, the modern tendency in lighting, both in the East and the West, has been an attitude of "the brighter, the better." Many new bath areas use florescent ceiling or wall-hanging fixtures that try uniformly to light up the entire area.

In fortunate contrast to the brightness of modern bathrooms, *onsens* often have lighting that takes advantage of the quiet shadows of the night. *Rotenburo*, baths that are placed in natural outdoor settings at *onsens*, are often allowed to remain dark at night, only illuminated by low-lit warm spotlights and with *andons*, lantern-shaped lighting fixtures, placed sparely in the adjoining garden. Originally, *andons* were made of wood, iron, or brass covered with *shoji* paper. Inside, rush-reed wicks placed in rapeseed oil would be lighted to cast a gentle glow. It is common today, however, to see *andon* made with glass or plastic in place of the *shoji*, and electric lightbulbs in place of the wicks and oil.

The idea to be learned today from the hot springs is to minimize the difference of brightness between the bath and the garden. If the bathroom is well lit and the garden is dark, one's world is narrowly confined to the interior of the bathroom. When the garden becomes softly lighted (and the bathroom softly darkened), then shrubs, trees, fences, and stones become visible, the world opens up, and the bather is transported to places distant. At night, then, consider for the interior of the bathroom using diffused lighting, having a mixture of electrical and nonelectrical. The use of flickering candlelight or a small oil *andon* creates a room that is warm and tranquil and in harmony with the world outside.

For daytime use of the bathroom, it might be enough to merely use the light that comes in from the outside. The considerations then would be the direction the window faces, the path the sun takes across the sky, and the time of day that the bath will be used. For example, if the bathroom is to be used primarily in the afternoon, then one will want to have southern and western sunlight. The height of the window can also help determine the mood of the room. Placing a window up high can give a sunny, open feel to a room, while placing it down close to the floor can create a quiet restful mood.

After the heat of the bath, sipping tea next to the garden allows one to cool off.

Yuagari
(after bath)
and Yusuzumi
(enjoying the cool of the evening)

After a long day, especially a hot summer day, the custom in Japan is to rid oneself of the day's fatigue by bathing and then sitting down in a clean starched *yukata* and having a cold drink. A fan helps to cool one after the heat of the bath. The Japanese word for this custom is *yuagari*, and it is enjoyed as a time of luxurious repose—a time of doing nothing but sipping a cold drink and being idle and languid, of enjoying the heat at day's end and allowing one's worries to escape the body. In the Edo period, *yuagari* was a popular theme for writers and was often used for haiku and senryu.

Yuagari no	Resting after the bath
teni kumorikuru	the mirror in the hand
masu kagami	is getting cloudier with the steam

A Memory

Yusuzumi is similar to *yuagari* but is specifically an evening rest during the hot summer season; it is the perfect way to end a busy day after a long hot bath. My mother would often tell me about my great-grandfather, whom I never had a chance to meet. Being a wealthy landowner and a man of leisure, he loved to take a bath at four o'clock in the afternoon, wander into the kitchen, and get a tray of small pieces of grilled steak (unusual for that time in Japan!), which he had prepared earlier, and a bottle of warm saké with a small golden cup. Although, as a man of leisure, he never engaged in any other household activities, this little ritual he did by himself. Sometimes he would give one or two pieces to my mother, who tried to stay watching by his side. But this was, after all, a time for himself. Happily carrying his tray, he would disappear into the large garden of his home and sit by himself at the moon-viewing mound. He would slowly sip the saké, pouring one for himself and, I wonder, perhaps pouring another at times for the moon, which would be rising above his head.

45

Without Silence

Particular sounds, like scents, have the power to conjure up in one's memory specific times or distinct moods. And because sound is so ephemeral—a sound is made, it is there, and then it is not—it expresses the fragility of the moment. A sound that is nostalgic for most Japanese is the chiming of *furin*, or wind bells. Made of metal, clay, or glass, they are usually hung under the eaves. To catch the wind, an oblong piece of paper is attached at the end of a thread hanging from the bell. The small, pleasant sound that results is one associated with summer evenings and with *yusuzumi*. If there is anything that can give any definition to air, *furin* surely will by their gentle ringing. Stirred by the softest breezes, they bring to those sitting nearby a sense of evening's coolness after the heat of day.

Another sound resonant of the past is the chirping and twittering of insects that live in the garden. The Japanese love the music made by insects, and, not too long ago, it was common to see insect vendors arriving in the city from the countryside, carrying small caged insects to sell. Listening to them was traditionally an aesthetic activity; the Japanese used to hold insect-listening ceremonies as part of festivities at temples, shrines, or private homes. Tranquil insect sounds are a perfect complement to the contemplative time spent in the bath, especially the songs of crickets and *suzumushi* (grass lark)—distinct sounds of late summer since they can produce their beautiful clear ringing music only during the hottest days of August and early September. Toward the end of September, as the days get shorter, the sound of *suzumushi* becomes thinner and thinner, each one living out its life and disappearing into the silvery October mist.

A wooden waterspout designed and made by Hinoki Soken of Japan.

An idyllic
pond in a
northern
California
residence.

The gurgle of water trickling down the rocks into a pond outside is another restful sound. Evenings, the Japanese like to soak in the tub, listening to the comfortable repetitious music of the water murmuring over the stones in small rivers or creeks outside the bath. This creates a moment of perfection—perfect because it is so fleeting.

The Family Bathing

When I was about nine years old, I made what I considered then a great discovery about human character. It was in my family, as in most Japanese families, the custom to bathe together, and even on the odd occasions when I would begin bathing alone, by the time I started washing my back, my father or mother would come slipping in through the frosted-glass door to help me.

Even for a self-absorbed nine-year-old, it was impossible not to be aware of my mother's incredibly frantic way of washing my back. It wasn't that I didn't appreciate her kindness in washing me, but she was so frenzied in her movements that I would squirm and twist, trying to avoid her scrubbing. I felt as though I was the kitchen floor from which she was scrubbing out a stain. As with everything she did, she was stubborn and determined, and whenever I started my squirming, she would grab my shoulder and hold me down, always managing to finish her task at hand. My squirming and her determination became an established pattern; yet, almost always, we ended our battles in laughter. I remember with great fondness the sense of complete happiness I felt when, finished with the scrubbing and laughing, she would fill the bucket and splash me to rinse off the soap. I believe now there was something about her frantic, chaotic energy that was instilled in me by her washing, by her touch, by the happiness she gave me.

My father was completely the opposite. He was slow and methodical in everything he did, whether he was washing my back or carefully inking out a design on drafting paper. Compared to my mother, whose hands moved wildly in her passion for cleanliness, my father's hands went in strict parallel motions, up and down, left and right, moving slowly and with discipline, almost as though he was planing smooth a piece of cedar. He was so precise in doing this that I felt I needed to sit respectfully still, so our baths together were always peaceful and quiet. One night, as I washed myself all alone, I tried to move my hands like him and realized that my hands kept going in every direction with an energy that seemed uncontrollable. That was the night I suddenly realized, even though friends and family always said I took after my father, that inside I was my mother.

A sunken Japanese bath in a residence in northern California.

Now that I am older, I can move my hands slowly with a measure of restraint as I wash myself, and most of the time, I believe I am quite methodical. Then my mind wanders; I visit places far away, and when I return, my hands are scrubbing my legs, my face, my back with a fierceness and determination that could only have come from my mother.

Japanese *ryokans* provide both public and private baths, as with this modern two-person bath at Kaho Nigata, Japan

One carefully rinses before bathing in the Japanese *ofuro*.

Bathing Japanese Style

In the West, a bath is a place where one goes to cleanse the body; in Japan, it is where one goes to cleanse the soul. In America, the idea of getting in a tub to soak conveys either a bubble-filled luxury, an extravagant and indulgent alternative to the speed and efficiency of the shower, or a once-a-week pioneer-style necessity of avoiding body odor. When one bathes in Japan, it is about much more than cleanliness, though cleanliness is important. It is about family and community, the washing of each other's backs before bathing; about time to be alone and contemplative—time to watch the moon rise above the garden. The idea of taking time and care with one's bath in Japan is as important as taking time and care with the cooking and serving of dinner. Unlike in America, where speed and efficiency are valued (and in many states, the idea of water conservation), the Japanese make bathing a ritual—a prescribed order of rinsing, washing, and soaking that is passed down from one generation to the next, becoming an integral part of the society at large.

Japanese bathing is basically made up of four steps. First, after taking off one's clothes in the *datsuiba*, the bather steps into the washing area next to the bathtub and sits down on a small stool. It is usual here to dip one's hand into the hot water to check the temperature. Since the entire area is waterproof, one picks up a wooden bucket (unfortunately,

51

sometimes today it is made of plastic) and scoops hot water from the tub, pouring it over the shoulders. This is repeated several times, rinsing off the dirt from the entire body. Rinsing is accomplished rather quickly, the point being twofold: to clean off the dirt from one's body before entering the hot water that is to be shared by others and to accustom the body to the temperature of the bathwater.

Now that the body is ready for soaking, the bather climbs over the edge of the bathtub and slowly descends into the bath. If the bathwater is too hot, cold water from the faucet can be added—though traditionally the Japanese bath is hotter than baths taken in America, usually tending to be about 110 degrees. One slowly sinks into the water, and after a while, the body becomes used to the water, feeling gradually as though the heat has penetrated to its core. The tingling sensation disappears and changes into a mildly dull pleasant feeling. Usually this is the sign that the body is ready to be scrubbed. In winter, this first soaking can take up to ten minutes; in summer, it can be as short as three minutes.

Feeling somewhat heavy, as if one has been cooked, the bather gets out of the tub and sits down on the stool again. This time he or she gets a bucketful of water from the faucet. Rubbing soap onto a loofah, washcloth, or sponge, he or she completely rubs him- or herself all over from head to toe. While still sitting down, the shampooing begins, and it is not unusual at this point for another family member to come in and help scrub the bather's back. The feeling is that now one has been cooked, it is time to vigorously scrub—to get every possible inch of dead skin and dirt scraped off the body. Most Japanese remain seated while soaping the body, taking care not to splash any soap scum into the tub water, and depending on mood, this scrubbing can take as long as ten to fifteen minutes.

The bather completely rinses off the soapsuds, then rinses once again. At this point, he or she is ready for the last soaking. Since the body is already warmed this time, it is easier to descend into the clean water. The body feels smooth and soft after the vigorous scrubbing, and the muscles and nerves begin unwinding from the accumulated tensions of the day. After this last soak, one might take a cold shower or simply splash some cold water over the shoulders. In the *datsu-iba*, the bather dries off and puts on a *yukata* or other comfortable clothing. Finally, the Japanese bath is finished and the rest of the evening awaits.

Taking a short bath is looked down upon—in Japan it is taking a *karasu no gyozui*, or raven's bath, with the implication that it is done hastily and without care. The Japanese put the American shower into this category. Bathing is to be done with care, taking time and pleasure, and should be valued as a prescribed part of one's daily routine.

A blue cotton *yukata* is traditionally worn during the warmth of summer evenings.

With and Without Clothing

The Japanese have many stages of undress around the bath—from the time of shedding one's clothing to holding (when in public) a washcloth over one's private parts, to putting on a *yukata* after the bath. It is almost as though one sheds the worries of the world as he or she undresses, and then, finally, relaxed and refreshed, relishes the carefree nature of the *yukata*.

For many Japanese there is no more ideal clothing than the *yukata*. It evokes a sense of perfect yet ephemeral moments, such as when seated after a hot bath along a wooden *engawa* and briefly feeling a soft cool breeze upon the face—like that first sip of a warm bitter saké after snow has fallen.

Historically, the *yukata* was a special garment worn for bathing, called a *yukatabira*. Following Buddhist tenets, people were instructed to wear this garment of cotton, silk, or linen for the maintenance of public morals. Wearing it helped bathers to avoid physical contact in a communal bath. Also worn fresh after the bath, it was used for drying the body in place of towels. Since this garment was cumbersome to wear during bathing, around the thirteenth century male bathers began using *yu-fundoshi*, or loincloths, and female bathers wore *yumaki* or *yumonji*, cloths that could be simply wrapped around one's torso. The custom then was that bathers would wash these garments in the tub, but eventually this was thought to be unhygienic, so, by the time of the Edo period, it finally became acceptable to bathe in public without clothing.

Wearing a yukata, a bather walks towards an outdoor bath at Ten Thousand Waves, Santa Fe, New Mexico.

As for the *yukatabira*, after it lost its original function, it metamorphosed into the *yukata*, made of cotton and worn during the summer days of heat. Often made of indigo cloth dyed with patterns of waves, flowers, insects, fish, calligraphy, or geometric shapes, the *yukata* is simple in appearance and comfortable in hot weather. Many people wear it today when they go to see a display of summer fireworks by a lake or river, or when they attend the local *obon matsuri*, the summer festival in their neighborhood shrine. And they wear *yukatas* on their way to the *sento*. Traditional inns also provide them for the overnight visitor, who, after a long soak, will stroll into the town in search of a cool breeze and merriment. In Japan, when one sees the sight of children in *yukatas* and hears the clip-clop sound of their *geta* sandals echoing around the corner, it is apparent that the long summer is almost over—soon to be followed by the typhoon season and crisp autumn weather.

An outdoor bath at Ten Thousand
Waves, Santa Fe, New Mexico.

The sunset lights the interior of a bath
in a northern California residence.

The Time of Day

It is said that when Japanese men return home from work, they ask two questions as soon as they walk in the door: "When will dinner be served?" and "Is the bath ready?" Japanese traditionally bathe in the evening, unlike Americans with their morning showers. There are good reasons for this; a bath relaxes one, removing him or her from the confusion and clutter of the day, and it induces a restful slumber. However, bathing right before sleep should be done in lukewarm water. In technical terms, it better stimulates the parasympathetic nervous system and accelerates the secretion of nor-adrenaline—in nontechnical terms, it lowers the level of psychological tension and physical stimulation, thus helping to shut down the entire body system before going to sleep. Conversely, if a person wants to wake up in the morning, a quick hot (not lukewarm) or cold shower/bath is recommended since it stimulates the sympathetic nervous system and accelerates the secretion of adrenaline, getting one ready to face the rush of the day.

But the Japanese take an evening bath to relax and feel refreshed after a long day at work. It acts as a transition between work and leisure, between public and private time. In Japan, schoolchildren and working people come home and take their baths fairly soon and only then sit down to eat dinner. It is also a wonderful chance for family members to relax together at day's end. Since the Japanese typically have only one bathing facility, preteen children often take their baths with their parents. This is a time spent chatting about the day, feeling relaxed together, and being close to each other. A side benefit comes in the morning, when the children are clean and ready to go to school and there is less tension for the parents, who, as in America, are rushing to get themselves ready for the day.

In short, bathing has assumed a more vital role in Japanese family life than merely cleansing oneself. Until recently, when the fad for morning showers became popular among young Japanese women, the

An outside woodstove heats the water for this California bath.

idea of morning bathing was reserved for special occasions, such as the first day of the year, when it is important to start the new year with a clean mind and body. It was also considered beneficial after a night of heavy drinking when one wanted to rid alcohol from the system. And it was also a practice to bathe in the morning when visiting *onsen*, or hot-spring resorts, where one bathes in the morning, the afternoon, the evening, late at night—three and sometimes four times a day, enjoying the medicinal hot waters as much as possible. Nothing is more luxurious than waking up in the morning in a *yukata* after a restful sleep and going down to the big communal bathroom, throwing off the *yukata*, opening the glass door, rinsing the body, and sinking into the hot bathwater while looking out at the purple mountain silhouette in the distant mist. As one watches, the silhouette becomes greener and crisper as the morning mist is burnt off by the emerging sunlight—and one's mind becomes cleared by the hot water and ready for the day ahead.

A Japanese bath allows the bather to indulge in the abundance of water.

Food and Drink

You have traveled into the mountains to a hot-spring resort—it is midwinter and snow is threatening to fall by night. You are greeted at the entrance of the *ryokan* and escorted to your room. A maid offers you a tray of small sweet cakes and rice crackers, a specialty of the area, and she prepares and pours for you a small cup of hot green tea. You sit there, enjoy the snack, sip the tea, and chat awhile—the maid arranges your dinner plans, tells you about the room amenities, and informs you about the baths, the area, and what to look for if you go shopping. It is only then that you arise to go take your first bath in the hot spring.

There is a logic in this when you realize how the digestive system is controlled by heat. Bathing in lukewarm water stimulates the nervous system, which not only relaxes all the body parts but also increases your appetite. Thus, it is ideal to take a brisk lukewarm bath before a big banquet. But if the stomach is totally empty and you bathe too long, it will leave you feeling dizzy and weak; hence the practice of eating a small snack before entering the bath.

Unlike many American spas, Japanese hot-spring hotels and inns offer meals (dinner and breakfast), lodging, and the thermal springs as a package deal. You would no more consider going to an *onsen* to bathe without

Sensuality is feeling the
cool breeze on one's face
while soaking in hot water.

dining than having sushi without wasabi. The dinner is usually elaborate, starting with various small dishes of mountain shoots, fresh sashimi, grilled meat and fish, pickles, an egg dish, skewered vegetables, or tempura, and ending with a bowl of rice and miso soup, and dessert. Often the banquet takes place in your own room or in a dining hall divided by *fusuma* screens. You dine after you have had time to relax, bathe, and don your *yukata*. Then, after the heavy meal and drinks, this is the time when it is better to soak in a lukewarm bath rather than in a very hot one.

Too often it is saké or cold beer that you drink at bath time—especially at the *onsen*, but there are many healthy alternatives. Chilled green tea or plain water with a slice of lemon are very refreshing. Traditional noncaffeinated Japanese drinks that are suitable during or after the bath are *mugi-cha* (barley tea), *soba-cha* (buckwheat tea), and *ume-cha* (salt plum tea). With its pungent roasted flavor, *mugi-cha* is a drink especially favored in summertime by the Japanese. During the hot season, it is rare to find a refrigerator without a glass bottle of *mugi-cha* ready to drink. You will want to keep the body well hydrated in the bath even though you are immersed in water, because the body still perspires in the hot water. And sipping chilled tea or lemon water is a pleasant prelude to your bath.

The Sensuality of the Bath

You shut your eyes and you can smell the pine tree right outside the window. There is the slight tinkling of a *furin* hanging from the branches. In the far distance is the sound of water rushing over rocks in the stream. You open your eyes and step into the hot water of the old *hinoki* bath, slowly letting your body become accustomed to the temperature. You sink down and lean back against the age-softened wood; how many times through the years has it been scrubbed and then scrubbed again, you wonder. The colors in the room are the colors of the out-of-doors—soft green-tinted browns, a rich cream color that reminds you of fresh peaches and cream, and slate gray of the tiles. The only excitement comes from the dark blue and rust-colored *yukata* hanging in the corner from the wooden hook. You sip *mugi-cha* from a handmade *raku* cup, and you are free finally from the barrage of the noise that assails you in daily life, at one with the quietude of the world you have created around yourself.

Each of the senses is engaged when bathing. Bathing is essentially a sensual experience. One thinks of how incomplete an experience it would be to soak in a natural thermal spring in the wilderness of the Eastern Sierras of California while wearing a swimsuit. Uncomfortable with the naked body, thinking it both sacred and profane, many Americans are not able to distinguish between what is sexual and what is sensual.

In Japan, people of all ages in families and in neighborhoods still bathe together in public baths and wash each other's backs. For example, a Japanese man, a corporate manager, despite having his own bath at home, still puts on a *yukata* and *geta* on Sundays and walks slowly to the nearby *sento*, whistling as he goes, in order to share his bath with his friends and neighbors. More than planning to meet acquaintances there, he is enjoying a shared moment of pleasure in the washing away of all the worries and concerns of the week gone by. Japanese people—school children, office groups, and families—will visit hot springs in groups two or three times a year, realizing how as colleagues, friends, families, and acquaintances, they can discover more about each other in this way of sharing the hot bathwater together.

An outdoor bath at Sansui-so, Japan.

It was only in the 1970s and through the hot tub that Americans discovered anything equivalent to this sensuality of the Japanese bath. Today, unfortunately, it has too often become the custom to wear swimsuits when hot tubbing. When hot tubs first became popular, it was the new-found freedom of being naked in hot water together that attracted so many young and old to the huge redwood water tanks. Many hot springs still have this sense of sensuality, especially those far off the paved road without other amenities. But, yet, Americans still have a measure of guilt in the enjoyment of such sensuality—a narrowness that at times precludes enjoyment of the full measure of the bath.

Japanese Bath Words

Furo, or bath: According to Yanagita Kunio, an anthropologist, the word *furo* that is now used for bath originated from a similar word, *muro*, which referred to a natural steam cave where people went to cleanse themselves by sweating. This evolved into a sauna-like room constructed from wood where the steam entered either from an adjacent steam room or from directly underneath a wooden platform. After being steamed, a bather would go outside and scrape off the dirt, dead skin, and scum, using an item such as a bamboo leaf. A cold rinse would finish this whole process.

Furoshiki, or cloth that is wrapped around something in order to carry it: "Sparks of fire and fight are two flowers of Edo. So we put *furoshiki* under the futon. In case of fire, we threw pots and pans on the futon, wrapped them all in the mighty *furoshiki* and ran." The *furoshiki* is a multipurpose wrapping cloth developed in the late-seventeenth century, originally used to hold and carry anything needed for the bath to and from the *sento*—items such as a change of clothes, cosmetics, a washcloth, and buckets.

In the old days, it was the custom to dye the family crest on the cloth, but today that is rarely seen. It is still used for the bath today; its use has spread so that one might see older ladies, often dressed in kimonos, walking down the street, holding a gift or some purchase carefully wrapped in their *furoshiki*.

Yu, or hot water, sacredness: *Yu*, the *kanji* character for hot water, is said to have originated from another character with the same pronunciation that meant sacredness. As this connection shows, hot water was considered sacred—water being elevated to a high esteem of religious significance. Originally, *yu* denoted an iron caldron used for bathing; later, it was made of wood. Today the word *yu* (hot water) is used almost interchangeably with the word *furo*, but using *yu* connotes the bathing experience rather than the physical structure of the bath. For example, when people ask each other "How was the *yu*?" they are asking about the experience, not the bath itself, and so this is a more apt question than asking "How was the *furo*?"

Sukinshippu, or skin-ship, the camaraderie achieved through being naked together: There is an unwritten understanding among the Japanese that "skin-ship" and the sharing of the bath is one of the most effective ways of becoming true intimate friends. For example, when schoolchildren go on an overnight school trip, they share the bath together. Seeing each other naked, cooling off together, taking meals together, and sleeping in the same room, they deepen their friendship in an open, unaffected manner.

Making a Bath

You have waited until the time was right to begin work on building your bathing area. It was too important to rush. You have lived in your home now for several years and almost

unconsciously have chosen the location where you want to bathe—it is not the room with the toilet and sink next to your bedroom on the second floor—the view there looking out to the mountains is wonderful, but you have found yourself, several times a week, settling more comfortably into the back corner of the open deck behind your house, sipping a cup of tea alone or talking quietly with your spouse. The branches of an orange tree hang over the deck, and it is just

The bath-house at the Tassajara Zen Center in northern California.

three steps to the pathway that leads down to the gurgling creek. You choose wood to build your bath, knowing that it will not last as long as more-modern materials, but you like the way it feels after years of use. Already you have planted a small grove of black bamboo in the one direction that looks out to a neighbor's property—your bath space will remain private to you and your family. You are going to extend the roof of the house over the bath, a gabled extension held up by post-and-beam construction that will protect the bath from falling leaves, though you have a slight regret you will not feel the rain falling on you when you bathe. Windows will open wide on two sides, but you will leave the third side without sash open to face the orange tree. You want the garden to intrude upon the bath, the smell of the citrus, and possibly even some nasturtiums that will grow up and over the windowsill.

Sliding doors allow this bath to be opened up to the outdoors at the Tassajara Zen Center in the Santa Cruz Mountains, California.

Water can flow from this Port Orford cedar bath onto the tiled floor.

A step away from the bath, you will have an area to wash. The plumber has said he can drain the soapy water from the washing area into your septic system, but you decide to have the bathwater go into a separate gray-water system that can be used for the garden. This is good, as you plan to change the water every day or two: in your household there are four who will be bathing nightly. You will have a shelf for towels and hooks to hang yukatas. The only large decision yet to make is the way you will heat the bathwater. Will it be by wood in a convection system or by an on-demand propane system? Either will work and each is with its own advantages. These are not decisions you want to rush.

Modern materials
are used to create a
traditional aesthetic
in this bath.

Materials

A bather settles herself into the bath; she is seated, not lying down as she would in a Western tub, and the water is over her shoulders, up to her neck. She looks out into the garden through the bamboo sudare, *then shuts her eyes. All she can feel is the heat of the water and the soft, almost furry, water-aged texture of the bath's* hinoki *cedar.*

Too rarely will one encounter this kind of bathing in today's Japanese homes. People's sentiments toward the bath are in two camps: the ones in the minority, who seek a traditional aesthetic and favor wooden bathing implements as well as the aged-cedar their bath is made from, and the majority, who seek convenience and practicality and are first in line for the latest technological innovations. The former are connoisseurs of materials drawn from nature, wood, marble, and granite. They understand that wood, when aged with water, is soft and warm to the touch and that modern synthetic materials can never equal its fragrance. They know the profound depths of marble and granite and how difficult it is to equal them using the

A traditional Japanese stainless-steel bath creates a modern aesthetic in this California home.

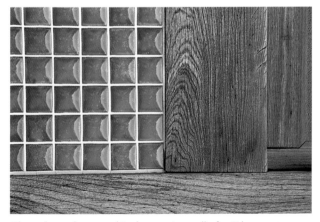

Tile and wood are used in the exterior wall of a Tokyo *sento.*

newer artificial materials. The latter group pursues the most-up-to-date innovations, purchasing for their homes the newer unit-baths made from all-purpose FRP (fiberglass-reinforced plastic) or from imitation marble. There is no question that these new materials are durable, light, easy to handle, and extremely easy to keep clean and sanitary. The cost, as well, is often less than for natural materials. Whereas marble and stone are cold, and one desires

heat in the bath, these newer forms of artificial marble, made of acrylic or polyester resin, have an exceptional ability to heat quickly and retain the warmth. But a bath is not about economics, and there are many that would argue it should not be about convenience. A bath is more than that; it is about one's inner self—his or her relationship to nature and to the society beyond.

Though this is the trend in the home, one can find hope in the nostalgic desire of the Japanese to visit hot-spring resorts. At *onsen*, the bathing tradition continues, and various kinds of cedar, stone, granite, and bamboo are used. When visiting resorts throughout Japan, bathers can find endless variations on the bathing space—many evocative of times past and still in touch with nature. These bathing spaces are creative and exquisitely crafted, where one can relax and settle the mind into a peaceful repose. Rustic baths in the countryside are shaped by large pieces of granite, varied in size and shape, creating a pool that suggests a running brook. Or in a more urban locale, bathers might find a *hinoki* wood tub, its smooth surface glowing quietly from behind billows of rising white steam. One goes to some baths simply to sit, soak, and look out onto Mount Fuji—the tub being carefully positioned so that he or she can see the reflection of the snow-covered peak in the water. Convenience may rule the household, but given the chance, it is to the past and a more natural world that most Japanese turn.

About Wood

In the crafting of a Japanese bath, the wood most revered is a type of cedar called *hinoki*. Especially venerated is the *hinoki* grown in the mountain region of Kiso in central Japan. Known for its straight and stable grain and beautiful light-

colored surface, it has been used through the years in the building of shrines, temples, and traditional homes. Containing the natural essential oil *hinokitiol* that prevents mold and mildew, this fragrant wood is especially suited for both the tub and the area sur-rounding it. Other woods that have been commonly used are *sawara* (saward cypress), *maki* (Chinese black pine), and *sugi* (cedar).

The great American counterpart to *hinoki* is Port Orford cedar, the majority of which is exported to Japan because of its excellent grain, surface, durability, and fragrance.

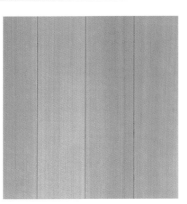

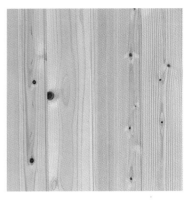

A mixture of materials is used in the simple construction of this Japanese bathhouse outside Grass Valley, California.

One would no more paint hand-planed cedar than use Kobe beef for dog food. When wood is used in Japan, especially after being finished by hand planing, traditionally the surface is left unfinished. Partially, this is a result of using *hinoki* wood, which contains a high dose of an essential oil that keeps it moist naturally, but there is also a feeling in Japan that bare wood left natural is more expressively beautiful than if it is painted. The wood that is used in the making of a bath is carefully chosen, and each plank is carefully planed over and over again until it attains a glistening, silky finish. Since Japanese carpenters plane along the grain, the finished result is much finer than any finish that could be applied; it is more than can be achieved by even the finest sandpaper.

The beauty of wood treated this way adds much to an interior. Its warm, soft yet crisp tone is beyond expression. If examined through a microscope, one can see that light reflects randomly off its surface as compared to the smooth surface of plastic or artificial marble, which reflects light in one uniform glaring direction.

Beyond aesthetics, there are many reasons to consider using natural wood. One is its ability to retain heat; on cold winter nights, the wooden slats on the floor in the washing area help keep

Port Orford cedar is used for both the tub and the lid in this bath built by East Wind (Higashi Kaze) Inc., of California.

a bather's feet warm. It also absorbs shock better than plastic or marble and feels soft when it is walked on with bare feet. And it is fragrant. The pervasive aroma of *hinoki* defines a traditional Japanese home for many. The aroma of the wood comes from the oils contained within. Not only does the oil help preserve the wood from insects, mildew, and mold, but some recent scientific research shows a positive effect on human health. In a recent study, when two groups of subjects were instructed to take a bath daily, the first group bathed in water with a type of essential plant oil, alpha-pinene, and the second group bathed in water without it. The first group recorded a positive increase of white-blood-cell count after only four weeks.

Wood and Water

The care of wood that has daily contact with water is not difficult. Most of what needs to be done is common sense. Since the surface of a Japanese wooden tub is not sealed by lacquer, you should avoid putting metallic objects in the tub that can cause rust. Do not use chemicals, soap, and bath salts since they may ruin the wood, and it's important not to use too harsh of a brush to clean a wooden tub. Instead, use a soft sponge or loofah to preserve the surface. Since wood shrinks when dry, it is a good idea that you use the tub regularly, or at least rinse it daily. An alternative is to keep several inches of water in the tub and change it periodically.

Oranges float in this bathwater, mirroring the Japanese winter tradition of the *yuzu* bath, when Japanese citrus fruit is put into the water.

If your tub is not to be used for a while, a tightly covered bucket of water can be placed inside the tub. Too much moisture, though, can cause problems of mildew and mold, so it is advisable to drain the water after bathing and to rinse the tub quickly. Keep the room well ventilated with open windows, but be careful not to have a wooden bath in direct sunlight. Many Japanese manufacturers recommend a check-up every several years. Even though a wooden bath is not as durable as one made of fiberglass, wood is a living material that ages beautifully as it is being used. And as it ages, your relationship with the bath deepens. Without question it is more work to have a wooden tub, but it is also an experience with great rewards.

An outdoor bath at the Hogetsu Inn in Hakone, Japan.

A Japanese bath in the winter
snow at Gorokaku, Gumma
Prefecture, Japan.

The Splash of the Water:

Planning and Constructing a Waterproof Room

The pleasure of the Japanese bath is in the feeling of abundance. Unlike the Western bathroom, where bathers take care not to spill or splash water beyond the tub, bathing in a Japanese *ofuro* means stepping carefully into the steaming hot bath, lowering oneself gradually, and feeling the luxury of having an overflow of water cascade out onto the floor. This sense of abundance is played out to its fullest at Japanese hot-spring resorts. Water is seemingly everywhere at these *onsen*—from the outdoor bath set among boulders of granite and next to the raging river to the quiet indoor *hinoki* bath next to enormous windows overlooking the distant mountain greenery.

A primary goal of constructing a Japanese bathroom is the creation of a space for relaxation. Most Japanese bathing areas are entirely waterproof and are composed of two areas: the actual tub used for soaking, and a washing area outside the tub for scrubbing and rinsing off soap. Sitting within this space, one does not have to worry about splashing water while using the handheld shower or flooding the floor with overflow from the bathtub. But one must always be careful about soap, which is never taken into the tub. Water is enjoyed here in its fullest abundance.

Water overflows from this stainless-steel bathtub.

A *hinoki* unit-bath manufactured by Hinoki Soken in Japan.

The contemporary domestic bathroom in Japan takes up anywhere from as little as twenty to about thirty-six square feet—just enough room for the tub and the washing area, with a space-saving sliding door separating the washing room from the *datsuiba*. Though variations exist, a typical tub size in Japan is about four feet long by two-and-a-half-feet wide and two feet high. Protruding out from the wall above the tub are hot- and cold-water faucets. In the washing area, a second set of faucets used for rinsing is usually set about eighteen inches off the floor—quite low to the ground. The handheld showerhead usually has two places it can be set, at about thirty-five inches and at sixty inches from the floor. Usually only one drain is set in the floor. The water from the tub drains out onto the washing area and down the floor drain.

Japanese-style bathrooms have distinctly low proportions as compared to those in the West. Since washing takes place while sitting down on a stool in a Japanese *ofuro*, rather than standing up as in an American shower, most of the activity occurs at a lower eye level. Hence, all the proportions for the mirror, the handheld shower, the windows, and the faucets are lowered appropriately. Deciding on the window height, for example, when seated on the stool, one should be able to have a view that looks directly outward rather than directed upwards. Having to look up can make a bather feel trapped in a cage. A recent innovation in Japanese bath-making is to embed the tub into the floor so as to overcome the difficulty of climbing in and out of a deep soaking tub. Typically when this is done, a twenty-four-inch tub will be sunk twelve inches, making it safer to step into yet allowing bathers to soak all the way up to their necks.

The focal elements of the garden are kept at the eye level of the bather in this hot-spring bath in Yunogomura Inn, Shuzenji, Japan.

Sunoko, the wooden slats used on the floor, keep a bather's feet warm when stepping into or out of the bath.

The Tools of Bathing

Through the years, many accessories for the bathroom have been developed in Japan. For example, a bucket, whether wooden or plastic, is indispensable. After many years of use and experimentation, the shape and size of these buckets have been standardized. There are two shapes. The first is without a handle and is about nine inches in diameter and five inches deep. This size is perfect; it is not too small to put both hands inside to wash and not too large and bulky to pick up with one hand and scoop out water from the tub. The other sort of bucket comes with a handle and is about six inches in diameter and five inches deep. For those Japanese who cannot afford a costly wooden tub, a wooden bucket at least gives a traditional ambience to the bathroom, not to mention the scent of cedar.

A stool made of wood or plastic is also important. At a glance, it looks too small for an adult to sit on, but it works well in the small area of the bathroom. Stools come in both round shapes and square shapes; the square ones have tops that are only about ten inches wide and six inches deep while the height is as low as six inches. Without this stool, bathing Japanese style would be very uncomfortable for the legs.

The *sunoko*, wooden slats, are another traditional implement that survives to this day. Originally used to let the steam come through in a steam bath, *sunoko* remained a traditional part of the *ofuro*. Today it is still used on the floor in the modern bathroom, especially when the floor is tile, slate, or concrete—in order to keep one's feet warm when washing. One can buy a premade *sunoko*

These traditional Japanese wooden buckets and seats are made by Ki Arts of Occidental, California.

at stores or install a custom-made one that takes up the entire floor space and can be taken out periodically for cleaning.

Sudare, screens made from bamboo strips, are not limited to usage in bathrooms, but they work wonderfully here to establish privacy and to control the sunlight glaring from outside. Since most Japanese gardens are meant to be looked at from a low angle—and in the bathroom this means from a sitting position in the washing area— a lowered *sudare* would not obstruct the view and yet would provide some measure of privacy. And because there are tiny slits of light between the strips of bamboos, air and light can be filtered in.

The lid is also part of the Japanese bath. Since family members in Japan use bathwater successively, to keep the water hot it is necessary to put the lid on between uses. Lightweight plastic ones are commercially available, but just a set of three or four pieces of wood across the tub can do the job.

A washcloth is used not only for washing before bathing but also, when in the bath, to soak with cold water and place upon the head to keep cool.

One can either shower before bathing in this Santa Fe bath or sit on the stool and wash in a traditional Japanese style before sinking into the hot water of the tub.

Light fills the quiet
space of the all-
wooden hot-spring
baths at Otakinoyu,
Kusatsu, Japan.

The Community of Bathing

When I first lived alone in Tokyo in an apartment complex without a bathroom, I found myself going with great pleasure every day to the neighborhood *sento*. It may have been the darkness of the cold evening streets that made me feel I needed to rush there to get warm, or it may have been my loneliness from living alone for the first time that made me want to see faces and hear people talking as night came on, but it was always with great anticipation that I gathered together soap, washcloth, and shampoo, wrapping them in a large cloth, and began my walk to the *sento*. I remember when I was a schoolgirl how envious I was of my childhood friend who went each evening to the *sento* with her mother, the two of them walking side by side with their bundles of bathing items. I had to be content staying at home with the bath I shared with my sister and parents. Now, living alone, the *sento* I found was one place I could be with others and yet still be by myself. I found there several nodding acquaintances, and the *banto-san*, the bathhouse attendant, came to recognize me, but there was never more than a casual exchange of remarks about weather, health, and the bathwater that we were soaking in together. Between long soaks in the hot water, I would go on quietly about my business of washing my hair and body as the other ladies, both younger and older, would also scrub their bodies and busy themselves. Sometimes I was right next to somebody, and other times I found myself all alone, lost in a world of my dreams. I remember suddenly coming out of my own thoughts one time to realize how everyone was scrubbing his or her body with such an intense seriousness, and I liked that. I liked all of us sharing that moment of cleansing and the sense of belonging and comfortable acceptance we had for each other without ever having to say anything about it.

With all of us naked and bathing together, there was a sense that we were, after all, just humans—all trying to live as well as we could. Outside, some of us would wear high heels while others would carefully wrap themselves in kimono—yet here, we were who we were without all the layers of artifice and identity. I remember one evening covertly watching a middle-aged woman clean and wash her face that had been covered with heavy makeup. When I finally saw her face clean and scrubbed, suddenly I felt like telling her that it was beautiful, that she didn't need to cover it. Without clothes, we had nothing to hide behind. And with the hot water to share, we felt safe and happy.

Public baths in Japan form bonds of closeness among the residents of the neighborhoods they serve.

Bathing Together

If one asks a Japanese person about his or her most vivid childhood memories, often he or she answers that it was the time spent at the bath with parents or the trip to the hot spring. Bathing in the company of others creates a special fellowship resulting from the breakdown of social mores and hierarchies. The reward is the complete sense of freedom from social and physical constraint as one effortlessly floats in quiet and still water.

At his home in Tokyo, an energetic four-year-old boy waits for his father to come home so they can take a bath together after dinner. Called to bathe, he quickly rises, and as he leaves the dining room, a sudden quietness fills the room, though only for a little while. Soon he is laughing and talking to his father in the bath, reporting about his day, sometimes chanting, other times singing contentedly.

And, at the hot spring, seeing a middle-aged woman wash her mother's back is not rare, and one only wonders about the deep sentiments exchanged between them in this comfortable time of togetherness. This is the tradition of Japanese bathing—time spent soaking, sharing, cleansing, relaxing, separately or together—realizing that this is not just about bathing; it is about the very way we want to lead our lives.

In this wooden bathroom, every sound is muted while the steam rises from the surface of the medicinal waters of the hot-spring baths at Otakinoyu in Kusatsu, Japan.

Glossary

andon: a paper-covered lamp stand

datsuiba: changing room

Edo period: a period from 1600 to 1867 when Japan was ruled by the Tokugawa dynasty

engawa: a wooden porch

furin: wind bells made of glass, metal, or clay

furo: a Japanese bath

furoshiki: a cloth wrapper

hinoki: a fragrant Japanese cypress wood

kasuga doro: a tall, formal lantern

mugi-cha: barley tea

noren: a shop curtain, also a type of curtain used to obstruct unwanted sunlight and views

okigata doro: a ground-style low lantern

onsen: hot springs

rotenburo: an open-air bath

ryokan: a traditional Japanese inn

sento: a public bath

shakkei: "borrowed scenery," an ancient technique of landscape architecture used to connect the enclosed yard to the surrounding views

shibui: an aesthetic concept that has been developed around the tea ceremony, referring to a reserved, simple, and elegant yet rough quality

soba: buckwheat noodles

soba-cha: buckwheat tea

sodegaki: a low ornamental fence that butts out of the wall of the house

sudare: a reed screen or a bamboo blind

sunoko: a drain board often made of wooden slats

suzumushi: a bell-ring insect—scientific name: *Homoeogryllus japonicus*

tatami: straw matting

ume-cha: plum tea

washi: Japanese paper

yu: hot water, bath

yuagari: a moment after a hot bath

yukata: a cotton/linen robe traditionally worn for and after bathing that is used today as a summer robe

yukimi doro: a snow-viewing lantern

yusuzumi: enjoying the cool of the evening

A third-generation tub maker, Arai Shuichi, handcrafts a *hinoki* bucket to be used for washing.

Resources

Accessories and Miscellaneous

Dandelion
55 Potrero Avenue
San Francisco, CA 94103
415-436-9230

Hana Shoji and Interiors
1815 Clement Avenue
Alameda, CA 94501
510-523-1851
—Custom-made *shoji* screens

Hida Tool & Hardware Co., Inc.
1333 San Pablo Avenue
Berkeley, CA 94702
510-524-3700
www.hidatool.com
—Japanese woodworking tools

Japan Woodworking & Design
233 South Maple Avenue, Unit 5
South San Francisco, CA 94080
650-873-6175
—*Shoji* panels and doors

Soko Hardware
1698 Post Street
San Francisco, CA 94115
415-931-5510
—Japanese baths and products

Thousand Cranes
1803 Fourth Street
Berkeley, CA 94705
510-849-0501
—Futons, kimonos, and Japanese gifts

Architects, Craftspeople, and Designers

Len Brackett
East Wind (Higashi Kaze), Inc.
21020 Shields Camp Road
Nevada City, CA 95959
530-265-3744
www.eastwindinc.com
—Japanese house design and carpentry

Paul Discoe
Joinery Structures
2500 Kirkham
Oakland, CA 94607
510-451-6345
—Japanese house design and carpentry

Chadine Flood Gong
Chadine Interior Design
15910 Ravine Road
Los Gatos, CA 95030
408-354-0606
—Interior design with an Asian theme

Ron Herman, Landscape Architect
261 Joaquin Avenue
San Leandro, CA 94577-4709
510-352-4920 phone
510-352-4922 fax
rherman@rherman.com

Ki Arts
P.O. Box 631
Occidental, CA 95465
707-874-3361
www.sonic.net/~kiarts/muir.html
—Traditional Japanese woodworking

Kiso Artech
82-1 Narai
Hikawamura, Kisogun,
Nagano, 399-6303, Japan
0264-34-3303
—Custom houses and bathrooms

Bath Makers, Manufacturers, and Dealers

Americh
13208 Saticoy Street
North Hollywood, CA 91605
800-453-1463
www.americh.com
—A deeper tub called the Kyoto (68" x 68" x 22") is available here.

Hinoki-Soken
305-15 Sakashita
Sakashitacho, Ena-gun,
Gifu, 590-9232, Japan
0573-75-5400
www.matrics.or.jp/hinokisoken/
—Bathtub and bathrooms made of *hinoki* wood

Paul Korhummel Design & Construction
P.O. Box 317
Inverness, CA 94937
415-663-9148

Robert's Hot Tubs
2343 Welcome Avenue
Richmond, CA 94804
510-234-7920
www.rhtubs.com/map.gif
—Handmade wooden bathtubs and hot tubs

Sea Otter Wood Works
Paradise Cove
Box 1268
Haines, AK 99827
www.woodentubs.com/about.html
—Handmade cedar tubs

Takagi Industrial Co. USA Inc.
23 Maychly, Suite 106
Irvine, CA 92618
949-453-8388
www.takagi-usa.com/web/bath.htm
—Deep soaking tubs and tankless water heaters

The Tubmakers
915 Ashby Avenue
Berkeley, CA 94710
510-843-2000
www.tubmakers.com
—Wooden spas, stoves, and saunas

Public Baths

Beverly Hot Springs
308 North Oxford Avenue
Los Angeles, CA 90004
323-734-7000
www.beverlyhotsprings.com/contact_us.htm
—Alkaline hot water spa with an Eastern touch

Gilroy Hot Springs
166 Geary Street #1209
San Francisco, CA 94108
415-434-2180
—Open by appointment only

The Golden Door
P.O. Box 463077
Escondido, CA 92046-3077
760-471-2393

Green Gulch Farm/Zen Center
Star Route #1
Sausalito, CA 94965
415-383-3986
—Meditation center and guesthouse with a Japanese bath

Kabuki Hot Springs & Spa
Japan Center
1750 Geary Boulevard
San Francisco, CA 94115
415-922-6000
www.kabukisprings.com

Orr Hot Springs
13201 Orr Springs Road
Ukiah, CA 95482
707-462-6277
—One of the most Japanese-style, *onsen*-like bath complexes in the United States

Osmosis Enzyme Bath and Massage
209 Bohemian Highway
Freestone, CA 95472
707-823-9231
www.osmosis.com
—Unusual enzyme baths and massages

Radisson Miyako Hotel San Francisco
1625 Post Street
San Francisco, CA 94115
415-922-3200
—Some guestrooms available with Japanese sunken baths

Shiatsu Rincon
7105 Gobernador Canyon Road
Carpinteria, CA 93013
805-566-9135

Tassajara Zen Mountain Center
300 Page Street
San Francisco, CA 94102
415-431-3771
—A rustic Zen retreat center with natural hot springs run by the San Francisco Zen Center in the Santa Cruz Mountains

Tea Garden Springs
38 Miller Avenue
Mill Valley, CA 94941
415-389-7123
www.teagardensprings.com

Ten Thousand Waves
P.O. Box 10200
Santa Fe, NM 87504
505-992-5025
www.tenthousandwaves.com

UCLA Hannah Center Japanese Garden
10920 Wilshire Boulevard, Suite 1520
Los Angeles, CA 90024-6518
310-825-4574
www.japanesegarden.ucla.edu
—Not for bathing, but a Japanese *ofuro* set in a garden setting

Watercourse Way
165 Channing Avenue
Palo Alto, CA 94301
650-462-2000
www.watercourseway.com